GW01180131

Original title:
Snowy Nights

Author: Lan Donne
ISBN HARDBACK: 978-9916-79-516-3
ISBN PAPERBACK: 978-9916-79-517-0
ISBN EBOOK: 978-9916-79-518-7

## Starlit Ballet of Frozen Fantasies

Under the moon's soft, silver glow,
Dancing shadows, whispers flow.
Swirling snowflakes, pirouettes bright,
A frozen stage in the still of night.

Figures weave in a frosty trance,
Nature's beauty, an elegant dance.
Stars above in a shivering spree,
Guide the dancers, wild and free.

A tapestry spun of shimmering light,
Each step painted in the quiet night.
Beneath the frost, dreams twirl and hide,
In this ballet, no need to decide.

The nightingale sings, soft songs it wakes,
Through crystal air, a symphony breaks.
Glistening trails on the cold, dark ground,
Echo the joy in each leap found.

As dawn approaches, the shadows wane,
Leaving traces of the night's sweet reign.
With every heartbeat, stories are spun,
Of the starlit ballet, now softly done.

## Dreams Covered in Ethereal White

In the silence of winter's embrace,
Dreams drift softly, a gentle trace.
Blankets of snow, pure as a sigh,
Whispers of wishes, floating high.

Clouds above in a hushed retreat,
Nestle the earth in their soft white sheet.
Every branch cloaked in delicate lace,
Holds the secrets of time and space.

Where the forest sleeps, dreams intertwine,
Sparkling softly, a glimmer divine.
Footprints hidden, like stories untold,
In the ethereal white, secrets unfold.

Petals of frost on the windowpanes,
Morning light dances, breaking chains.
As the world awakens, silent yet bold,
In every heartbeat, new tales are told.

Through the crystalline air, laughter rings,
Carried on breezes, the joy it brings.
Dreams covered in white, a canvas so bright,
Painting the dawn, a beautiful sight.

## Winter's Lullaby Under a White Veil

Snowflakes dance in the cold night air,
Whispers of dreams lie everywhere.
Silent shadows in moonlight creep,
Nature's stillness sings us to sleep.

Branches heavy with glistening white,
A world wrapped gently, pure and bright.
Soft breaths of winter, calm and clear,
A lullaby that draws us near.

Footsteps muffled on the soft ground,
Each moment paused, a sacred sound.
In this embrace, hearts find their way,
Peaceful twilight, end of day.

## Ethereal Silence of the Frosted World

In the stillness of a frozen morn,
Nature's beauty is gently worn.
Glistening crystals adorn each tree,
A tranquil vision, wild and free.

Breath of winter, crisp and bright,
Echoes linger in fading light.
Footprints trace where shadows play,
In this silence, thoughts drift away.

Frosted grasses in soft repose,
A tranquil symphony, silence grows.
Majestic calm in a world of white,
Wrapped in the arms of endless night.

## Evening Hush Beneath a Shimmering Sky

The sun dips low, painting the sky,
As the stars begin to softly sigh.
Whispers carried on the evening breeze,
Wrap around us like gentle leaves.

Nightfall cloaks the world in dreams,
In twilight's warmth, everything gleams.
Moonlit paths guide our way ahead,
Through shadows of what the day has bred.

Crickets serenade the cool dark,
Nature's lullaby, a soothing spark.
Beneath the starlit canvas high,
We find our solace, you and I.

## Frosted Leaves and Starlit Secrets

Leaves adorned in a crystal coat,
Whispers of autumn softly float.
Starlight peeks through branches bare,
In this moment, all fears lay bare.

Secrets held by the frozen ground,
Mysteries in the silence found.
Each flicker of light, a story spun,
In nature's quilt, we are as one.

The chill draws close, yet fires warm,
Encircling hearts with gentle charm.
In this tapestry of night and frost,
We gather memories, never lost.

## Illuminated by Winter's Chill

The moon hangs low and bright,
Casting shadows on the snow.
Frozen whispers fill the night,
As the cold winds gently blow.

Icicles dangle from the eaves,
Like crystal tears of winter's heart.
Nature rests beneath the leaves,
Tucked away, a work of art.

A blanket white, perfectly laid,
Softly covers all that's near.
In the silence, dreams are made,
In the frosty, fragile sphere.

# The Breath of a Frigid Night

Stars blink above, icy and clear,
The world exhales in frosty sighs.
Each breath a whisper, sharp and dear,
In twilight's grasp, where magic lies.

Snowflakes dance on the chilling breeze,
A ballet spun from winter's grace.
Nights like these, they aim to please,
A stillness found in time and space.

The air is thick with sparkling light,
As shadows lengthen, thin and bold.
Each moment holds a quiet might,
A tale of warmth in the cold.

## Solitude in a Crystal Realm

In the stillness, echoes fade,
Blanketed by a shimmering sheet.
Nature's beauty, a grand parade,
In this tranquil, wintry seat.

Frozen branches lace the sky,
Whispering secrets, soft and low.
In this realm, my thoughts can fly,
Like snowflakes dancing to and fro.

A crystal kingdom, vast and wide,
Embracing all in purest white.
In solitude, I choose to bide,
Finding peace in winter's night.

## Whispered Wishes in the Cold

Winds will carry dreams away,
Tender whispers, soft and true.
In the frost, the hearts will sway,
Underneath the starry hue.

Frozen wishes on the ground,
Captured in the glistening dew.
In this moment, dreams abound,
A world awaiting something new.

As the night drapes over me,
I close my eyes and start to see,
In the silence, hope runs free,
A winter's breath, my reverie.

## Frostfire

In the stillness, embers glow,
Sparkling under winter's show.
A dance of warmth in icy air,
Frostfire flickers, bright and rare.

Amidst the chill, a warmth ignites,
Whispers hidden in the nights.
Softly glowing, like a dream,
In the cold, we share our gleam.

## The Dance of Winter Spirits

In the moonlight, spirits glide,
Waltzing where the shadows hide.
Snowflakes twirl in playful glee,
Winter's dance, wild and free.

Around the pines, they swirl and sway,
Carving paths of silver spray.
Breath of frost in evening's grace,
Nature tells a sacred space.

## Celestial Frost against Dark Skies

Stars like diamonds, cold and bright,
Pierce the darkness of the night.
A canvas vast, where dreams reside,
Celestial frost, our hearts collide.

Beneath the shimmer, secrets flow,
In icy winds, the whispers grow.
Each breath a cloud, ethereal sigh,
In the stillness, we reach for the sky.

## Evening's Icy Palette

Brushstrokes of blue, white, and gray,
Paint the sky at close of day.
Winter hangs on nature's breath,
An icy palette, still as death.

Shadows shift in twilight's hold,
Stories woven, silently told.
The world adorned in frozen light,
As dusk descends, and stars take flight.

# The Hush of Winter Shadows

Snowflakes whisper, soft and slight,
Blanketing the world in white.
Silent trees, their branches bare,
Holding secrets in the air.

Footsteps crunch on frozen ground,
In this quiet, peace is found.
Nature sleeps, a tender sigh,
Beneath the vast and starlit sky.

Shadows dance in the pale moon's glow,
Frozen rivers cease to flow.
A gentle hush, the night holds tight,
Winter's magic, pure and bright.

Fires crackle, warmth we crave,
Echoes linger, soft and brave.
In this stillness, moments gleam,
Wrapped in winter's tranquil dream.

# Midnight's Icy Breath

Against the window, frost does paint,
A delicate, mysterious faint.
Beneath the stars, a chill awakes,
In every whisper, silence shakes.

Night's embrace, a tender grip,
Hushed like secrets on the lip.
Winds that sigh with icy grace,
Brushing softly, time and space.

Moonlight bathes the sleeping ground,
Where shadows weave, and dreams are found.
A kaleidoscope of winter's night,
Softly shimmering, pure delight.

Midnight whispers, secrets kept,
In the stillness, quietly swept.
This frozen breath, a fleeting lore,
Invites the heart to seek for more.

## Enchanted by Northern Lights

Dancing colors, vivid displays,
Twinkling through the night's embrace.
Mysteries of the Arctic skies,
Illuminate where magic lies.

Like ancient tales the heavens weave,
A tapestry that we believe.
Cascading hues in a cosmic dance,
Awakening dreamers lost in trance.

Underneath this colored shroud,
Nature sings her song aloud.
Echoes of the wild collide,
In every swirl, hope and pride.

Hearts aglow with a quiet fire,
Inspires whispers of desire.
Captivated by the cosmic light,
Finding peace in the endless night.

## Traces of Echoing Silence

Softly falls the evening shade,
Where silence lingers, thoughts cascade.
Footprints fade upon the path,
Whispers lost in nature's bath.

Gentle breezes weave between,
Echoes of what might have been.
Each moment holds a fleeting grace,
In this quiet, find your place.

Stars emerge, the night's soft crown,
Hiding dreams that swirl around.
There in darkness, secrets dwell,
In the silence, hearts compel.

Listen closely, hear the call,
Within the stillness, we are all.
Traces linger, soft and wise,
In echoing silence, true love lies.

## Whispers of Winter's Veil

In the hush of falling snow,
Whispers dance in twilight's glow.
Frosted trees, a silent choir,
Echo dreams from night to fire.

Beneath the stars, a blanket white,
Softly kissed by winter's night.
Footsteps trace a hidden song,
Where the chill winds wander strong.

Frozen lakes, a glistening guise,
Reflecting secrets in the skies.
Crystals form on barren boughs,
Nature bows in quiet vows.

In the warmth of fireside's grace,
We find our peace, a cherished place.
Winter whispers through the trees,
In every breath, a gentle freeze.

Time slows down, the world unwinds,
In this realm, our heart aligns.
With each flake that falls anew,
Winter's veil wraps me and you.

# Frost-Covered Dreams

Fields of white, a tranquil sight,
Frosted dreams take shape at night.
Underneath the silver moon,
Whispers chase the icy tune.

Each breath forms a spectral mist,
In the cold, we find the bliss.
Nature holds a quiet stare,
Magic lingers in the air.

Crystal shards on windowpanes,
Patterned dreams, sweet refrains.
Moonlit paths through silent woods,
Nestle deep in winter's moods.

As the dawn breaks soft and bright,
Frosted jewels catch the light.
Each echo tells a secret plot,
In this chill, we feel a lot.

From the depths of snow we rise,
Buoyant hearts beneath the skies.
In the frost, our stories gleam,
Awake within our winter dream.

# Moonlit Tranquility

In the stillness of the night,
Moonlight drapes the world in white.
Stars in patterns softly weave,
Tales of those who dare believe.

Whispers float on chilly air,
Carried dreams and fleeting care.
Trees stand guard with weary grace,
Offering the night a face.

Clouds drift by like softest sighs,
Drifting thoughts in velvet skies.
Peaceful moments stretch and fold,
Wrapped in secrets, soft and bold.

Footsteps crunch on fresh awake,
In this dream, we gently take.
Breath held close in winter's charm,
Every heartbeat, safe and warm.

As the dawn begins to rise,
We carry peace into the skies.
Moonlit dreams that softly fade,
In our hearts, they will cascade.

## Crystal Blankets of Silence

Underneath the silver skies,
Crystal blankets, nature's prize.
Frosted whispers quilt the ground,
Softly wrapped, we hear the sound.

Silent nights of deep embrace,
Calm reflections find their place.
Every flake tells stories old,
In their touch, a magic cold.

Glistening trails where shadows play,
Hidden secrets, night and day.
Each breath spoken claims its grace,
In the hush, we find our space.

Dancing lights of winter's breath,
Paint the world in shades of death.
Yet from this stillness rises life,
Nature's pulse, away from strife.

Wrapped in white, our dreams take flight,
In the silence, hearts ignite.
Crystal blankets, time stands still,
Through winter's charm, we bend to will.

## Frost-Laden Memories

In the stillness of the night,
Snowflakes dance like whispered light.
Each breath forms a frosty plume,
Echoes of winter in the gloom.

Branches bowed with crystal dreams,
Underneath the moon's soft beams.
Silence wraps the world in white,
Holding secrets out of sight.

Footprints trace a path of care,
In the chill of winter air.
Memories like snowflakes fall,
Delicate, yet they enthrall.

Time stands still in this embrace,
Frost-laden whispers interlace.
Nature's art, a fleeting sigh,
A moment's breath before goodbye.

## The Quietude of Winter's Blanket

Blanketed in white so pure,
Whispers of the frost endure.
Every corner holding peace,
As the world seems to release.

Quietude in frozen air,
A soft touch beyond compare.
Trees stand tall, yet softly sway,
In the hush of winter's play.

Crimson berries, a sight so bright,
Glimmering in the soft moonlight.
Silent footsteps on the ground,
In this haven, calm surrounds.

With each flake that gently lands,
Nature holds us in its hands.
Underneath this silent shroud,
Winter wraps the earth so proud.

## Glimmering Secrets of the North

Underneath the ancient stars,
Whispers travel near and far.
Tales of ice and frost unfold,
In the north where dreams are told.

Crystalline lakes shimmer bright,
Mirroring the frosty night.
Secrets hidden in the snow,
Ancient wonders lie below.

Dancing auroras, a vivid hue,
Painting skies in brightest blue.
Land of magic, bold and free,
Unraveling its mystery.

Footfalls echo through the pines,
In the woods that twist like vines.
Glimmers of life, all around,
In the silence, beauty found.

# Nightfall in a Shimmering World

As day gives in to night's embrace,
Stars awaken, taking their place.
The world transforms in silken glow,
Wrapped in beauty soft and slow.

Silver shadows softly creep,
In the stillness, secrets seep.
Moonlit paths invite the bold,
Stories waiting to be told.

Frosted breath hangs in the air,
Magic lingers everywhere.
Whispers of the night entice,
In this realm of cold and ice.

As darkness falls, the heart takes flight,
Exploring dreams in the fading light.
Nightfall casts its gentle spell,
In a world that gleams so well.

# Frozen Lullabies

In the stillness of the night,
Snowflakes dance in gentle flight.
Whispers of dreams begin to weave,
A soothing song to help believe.

Moonlit shadows softly creep,
Carrying secrets, lulled to sleep.
Nature hums a tranquil tune,
Underneath a silver moon.

Branches bow with icy grace,
Holding winter's warm embrace.
Each breath a cloud, a wish to share,
In this cradle, free from care.

Stars twinkle like diamonds bright,
Guardians of the silent night.
Cradled in the arms of peace,
Frozen lullabies never cease.

# Glittering Silence

In the hush of heavy snow,
Time stands still, soft winds blow.
Blankets white, a world anew,
Wrapped in stillness, calm and true.

Footsteps fade on frosted ground,
Echoes lost, no other sound.
Each flake falls with tender grace,
A fleeting touch, a warm embrace.

Stars reflect on icy streams,
Night unfolds in silver dreams.
Each moment, a crystal flash,
In the quiet, whispers clash.

A glittering fabric of the night,
Weaving shadows, pure delight.
In this realm where silence reigns,
Every heartbeat softly chains.

## The Beauty of a Winter's Canvas

A tapestry of white and grey,
Nature's brush in grand display.
Trees adorned with crystal lace,
In every corner, winter's grace.

Footprints sketch a fleeting tale,
Winds of winter, soft and pale.
Each horizon shimmering bright,
In the magic of muted light.

Mountains wear a cloak of silk,
Rivers freeze like cream and milk.
Sky dips low, a canvas vast,
In colors bold, a spell is cast.

Frosty air, a breath of art,
Whispers carried, nature's heart.
In this world, both fierce and calm,
Winter's beauty sings a psalm.

# Frosted Whispers

In the morning, soft and clear,
Frosted whispers fill the sphere.
Breath of winter on each tree,
Sharing secrets, wild and free.

Wind carries tales from afar,
Echoes of a wishing star.
A fragile world with silver sheen,
Nature's brush, so pure and keen.

Each petal cloaked in icy dew,
Crystals formed from skies of blue.
Life slows down, a gentle pause,
In this beauty, no flaws.

Frosted whispers weave a song,
Echoing where we belong.
In every twinkle, every sigh,
Winter's magic will not die.

## Silver Reflections

Under the moon's soft glow,
Ripples dance on the lake,
Whispers of dreams long past,
In silver fragments they wake.

Stars scatter in the night,
A tapestry so divine,
Each one tells a story,
Of lost moments in time.

The breeze carries secrets,
Through branches swaying free,
Nature's gentle reminder,
Of life's sweet melody.

In this tranquil stillness,
The heart finds its own beat,
Echoes of joy resound,
Where the sky and water meet.

Silver reflections whisper,
Of hopes and silent prayers,
A world wrapped in serenity,
Where the soul's peace repairs.

# Glacial Murmurs

Silent icebergs drift slow,
In a dance of frozen grace,
Each creak a distant story,
Of time's relentless chase.

The northern winds embrace,
With a chill that bites the skin,
Yet warms the spirit deeply,
As icy dreams begin.

Below the surface glimmers,
A world both bright and cold,
Nature's quiet beauty,
In shades of blue and gold.

In the heart of winter's chill,
Life holds its breath in awe,
Murmurs of ancient glaciers,
Giving silence its law.

Each thaw brings forth a sound,
A symphony of ice,
Whispers of glacial tales,
Wrapped in nature's voice.

## Under the Celestial Frost

Beneath the vast expanse,
Stars twinkle like bright seeds,
Night weaves its icy fabric,
To fulfill the heart's needs.

Frost kisses blades of grass,
With a touch so pure and light,
A blanket of glimmering shards,
Blankets all through the night.

The moon casts silver shadows,
Over valleys low and deep,
While the world lays quiet,
In a soothing, frozen sleep.

Galaxies spin in silence,
Whispering tales of old,
Lessons wrapped in starlight,
In mysteries yet untold.

Under this celestial dome,
Hearts find their way to soar,
Discovering hidden wishes,
On this frost-kissed floor.

# Ethereal Nightfall

As dusk unfolds its wings,
The world dons its cloak of grey,
A whispering serenade,
Guides the light away.

Soft shadows stretch and yawn,
While the sun bids warm goodbye,
Stars awaken from their slumber,
In the vast, unending sky.

The atmosphere is laden,
With dreams that softly bloom,
In the twilight's gentle grasp,
Dispersing all the gloom.

Each moment wrapped in magic,
As night blankets the earth,
A canvas painted softly,
With hues of silent mirth.

Ethereal nightfall beckons,
To wander through the dark,
With hope lighting the path,
Igniting every spark.

**Ghostly Footprints in the Wistful Snow**

In the quiet of the night,
Footprints whisper on the ground.
Silent tales of those in flight,
Lost in dreams, yet still around.

Frosty echoes call their names,
Shadows dance where no one goes.
Chasing shadows, playing games,
Tracing paths that time bestows.

Wistful sighs in candlelight,
Memories wrapped in white repose.
Glimmers of a past so bright,
Drift like feathers, soft as prose.

In the moon's embrace they glide,
Figures formed in fleeting glow.
With every step, they seem to hide,
In the beauty of the snow.

Yet as morning starts to break,
Footprints fade into the air.
All that's left is softly wake,
A ghostly tale beyond compare.

# Stars Adrift in a Sea of White

In the velvet of the night,
Stars are scattered, pure and bright.
Drifting gently in their play,
Whispers of the end of day.

Above the world, a crystal sea,
Twinkling lights in harmony.
Every star a distant song,
Calling out, where dreams belong.

Floating clouds, a soft embrace,
Casting shadows, tracing space.
Moonlight bathes the earth below,
As silent breezes start to flow.

Each star shines with tales untold,
In the dark, their secrets hold.
Guiding hearts with gentle grace,
Leading souls to timeless space.

When the dawn begins to break,
Stars retreat, their magic fades.
In their wake, a quiet ache,
For the light that softly cascades.

## Frosty Kisses Beneath the Moon

Beneath the moon's enchanting glow,
Frosty kisses fall like dew.
Whispers carried on the snow,
Promises, old yet so new.

Chill of winter in the air,
Every breath a misty sigh.
Covered paths, we've walked with care,
In this world of white, we fly.

Frozen moments, yours and mine,
Captured in the frosty light.
Hearts entwined, a love divine,
Dancing softly through the night.

Each twinkling star, a witness true,
To the vows that softly spark.
Underneath the sky so blue,
Love ignites within the dark.

When dawn breaks, we'll still remain,
Echoes of our soft embrace.
Through the frost and through the pain,
Love's sweet kiss will leave its trace.

## Frostbitten Dreams Under a Starlit Canopy

Underneath a starlit dome,
Frostbitten dreams begin to rise.
In the night, we find our home,
Guided by the cosmic ties.

Glistening like diamonds rare,
Memories twinkle in the air.
Wanderers in a silent land,
Finding warmth in shadows' hand.

Each frosty breath, a whispered plea,
Carried forth on winter's breeze.
Holding on, just you and me,
Entwined in the night's sweet tease.

Out of dreams, our laughter flows,
Rising with the morning light.
In the frost, our love still glows,
Wrapped in warmth, a pure delight.

Beneath this vast and endless sky,
Frostbitten dreams take flight once more.
Together, we will always try,
To find what fate has in store.

# Moonbeams on a Frozen Canvas

Moonlight spills on snow so bright,
Whispers dance in the pale night.
Stars twinkle in their silent glee,
Painting dreams for you and me.

Frozen lakes reflect the glow,
Nature's wonder, soft and slow.
Silver shadows gently play,
Guiding us along the way.

Frosted branches hold their breath,
Silent stories of quiet death.
Yet within the cold, there's peace,
In this stillness, find release.

Snowflakes swirl in a fluent waltz,
Each unique, without faults.
They settle down, a soft embrace,
In their fall, we find our space.

As the night begins to fade,
Moonbeams dim, but dreams cascade.
In their light, we weave our hopes,
In frozen realms, our spirit copes.

# Crystal Lattice of the Night

Beneath the stars, the world awaits,
A crystal lattice, nature's gates.
Frosted whispers in the breeze,
Carry secrets through the trees.

Icicles hang like silver swords,
Glistening sharply, nature's words.
Each breath clouds in the chilly air,
Tales of magic everywhere.

The moon above casts graceful lines,
In frozen patterns, time aligns.
Each sparkle sings a lullaby,
To the night, a gentle sigh.

Underneath this sparkling veil,
Silent stories start to unveil.
In the stillness, hearts combine,
Lost in the beauty, all is fine.

When morning comes, the frost will fade,
Yet memories of the night are laid.
In every diamond on the ground,
A magic in silence found.

# The Stillness of a Frigid Evening


The stillness wraps the world in white,
Veils the earth with calm delight.
Every sound is hushed and low,
In this quiet, we can grow.

Branches bow with frosty weight,
Nature holds its breath, so great.
In the air, a chill ignites,
Bringing peace on frigid nights.

Stars above in frozen dance,
Glimmers cast a fleeting glance.
While shadows stretch across the land,
We reach out, and take a stand.

Moments linger, time stands still,
In the quiet, feel the thrill.
Embrace the beauty of the cold,
As winter's tales unwritten unfold.

Each breath speaks of thoughts untold,
In the cheers of nights so bold.
Together we weave our dreams anew,
In the stillness, just me and you.

# Frosted Tales in the Silence

Frosted tales in silence lay,
Whispering secrets of yesterday.
Underneath the starry cloak,
Dreams emerge, softly spoke.

Winds caress the frozen ground,
In this stillness, solace found.
Every flake a story wrought,
In each twinkle, hope is sought.

Branches glisten with a sheen,
Nature's beauty, so serene.
As shadows stretch with every sigh,
The night unfolds, and we comply.

Through the chill, our hearts ignite,
Burning bright in the polar night.
In the quiet, friendships bloom,
Chasing away the creeping gloom.

With each breath, the frost unfolds,
Every tale in the silence told.
Together we find warmth within,
In iced songs, our love begins.

## Nighttime's White Symphony

In the hush of night sky,
Snowflakes dance, gently sigh.
A soft whisper on the ground,
As dreams and silence abound.

Moonlight casts a silver hue,
Stars twinkle in the deep blue.
The world wrapped in a soft quilt,
Nature's peace, no dreams unspilt.

Through the trees, the shadows creep,
In their arms, the secrets keep.
Winter sings a tranquil song,
In this moment, we belong.

Footsteps crunch on frozen ground,
In this stillness, joy is found.
As I wander, thoughts take flight,
In nighttime's symphony, pure delight.

A canvas painted soft and bright,
Where every heartbeat feels just right.
I lose myself in crystal light,
Embracing magic of the night.

# The Language of Frost

Frosted breath on window panes,
Whispers of the chilly rains.
Each crystal tells a story clear,
Of winter's grip, its magic near.

Patterns form like fleeting dreams,
Nature's art in silver beams.
Delicate as fleeting time,
Frost awakens quiet rhyme.

Cold fingers touch the earth's face,
Blanketing the world in grace.
Softly, gently, winter speaks,
In every crevice, frost seeks.

Underneath the pale moonlight,
Frost's embrace holds stars so bright.
In the silence, secrets flow,
Tales of beauty few may know.

Every breath, a cloud of dreams,
In icy whispers, hope redeems.
The language of frost unfolds slow,
A wondrous world where feelings grow.

# The Stillness Beneath the Stars

Beneath the stars, the world sleeps,
In the stillness, silence creeps.
Gentle winds brush through the trees,
Carrying whispers, soft as these.

The moonlight bathes the earth in glow,
Lighting pathways, soft and slow.
Each twinkle tells a secret old,
In the night sky, tales unfold.

Shadows dance on snowy fields,
Nature breathes, her power yields.
Every heartbeat, calm and neat,
In this stillness, life feels sweet.

The world above, so vast and wide,
In cosmic ocean, we reside.
We find our peace in moonlit grace,
Under stars, we find our place.

In the quiet, dreams take flight,
Guided by the soft starlight.
The stillness soothes both heart and mind,
Within this night, true peace we find.

# Enveloping Beauty of the Cold

A frosty breath adorns the trees,
Winter's touch, a gentle tease.
Nature's beauty, crisp and bright,
In the cold, a world of light.

Snowflakes fall like whispered dreams,
Turning earth to silver seams.
Every corner dressed in white,
In the cold, the world ignites.

The air, a canvas fresh and clear,
Bringing forth the joy and cheer.
Silent nights, where magic grows,
In every flake, true beauty flows.

Icicles hang like nature's art,
Each glistening, a beating heart.
In the cold, life finds its soul,
Embracing beauty, making whole.

Through the chill, our spirits rise,
Wrapped in warmth beneath the skies.
In the embrace of winter's hold,
We find the love, the tales untold.

# Frost-kissed Serenade

Under the moon's soft gleam,
Whispers of winter stream.
Blankets of snow unfold,
Tales of the night retold.

Crystals on branches sing,
Nature's serene offering.
Echoes of laughter play,
In the frost's gentle sway.

Stars twinkle with delight,
Guiding the hearts to light.
Each breath like a soft plume,
Awakens the winter's bloom.

Fires crackle near and dear,
Shadows dance, drawing near.
In this frosty serenade,
Love's warmth won't ever fade.

So let the night unfold,
As dreams begin to mold.
In the crisp, serenade's tune,
Hearts merge with the moon.

# Shadows Dance on Icebound Streets

Beneath the starry sky,
Whispers drift and sigh.
Footsteps on frosty ground,
Echoes of joy abound.

Shadows stretch and glide,
Together, side by side.
Laughter fills the cool air,
Moments we gladly share.

Candles flicker with cheer,
Casting warmth near and dear.
Figures twirl with delight,
In the heart of the night.

Icebound paths gleam and shine,
A canvas, pure and fine.
Every glance, every chance,
In the shadows we dance.

With each turn we embrace,
Frosted breath in our chase.
Creating new memories,
Underneath the frosty trees.

## Glistening Stars in a Crystal Heaven

Glimmers in the night sky,
Twinkling gems up high.
A canvas, dark and deep,
Where ancient dreams do sleep.

Each star, a story spun,
Under the watchful sun.
Whispers of dreams untold,
In heavens bright and bold.

Crystals shimmer and gleam,
Starlight weaves a dream.
Floating on evening's breeze,
Time gently drifts with ease.

Hearts lifted to the skies,
Counting the constellations' ties.
In this cosmic embrace,
We find our rightful place.

With each breath, we behold,
A tapestry of gold.
In this serene expanse,
We find our souls' true dance.

# Whispering Winds of the Frozen Dusk

As daylight fades away,
Whispers come to play.
Chill of the evening air,
Tender moments to share.

Winds that softly sing,
Bringing warmth to the spring.
Echoing hopes anew,
In a world painted blue.

Snowflakes drift and fall,
Nature's gentle call.
In the hush of the night,
Dreams take their flight.

Stars awaken with grace,
In the nighttime's embrace.
As shadows gently sway,
We cherish the day.

In the dusk, we connect,
With all we reflect.
Whispering winds will guide,
As love walks beside.

# The Night's Silver Coat

The moon hangs high in velvet sky,
Its glow a whisper, soft and shy.
The stars like diamonds gently gleam,
In winter's grasp, a silvery dream.

Snowflakes dance on chilly air,
Blanketing the world with care.
Each breath a cloud of frosty white,
As night unfolds, a pure delight.

Crisp shadows stretch on frozen ground,
In silence, only peace is found.
The night unfolds its soft embrace,
A tranquil magic, time and space.

Trees adorned with crystals bright,
Stand guard beneath the moonlit light.
Nature whispers, calm and slow,
In the night's enchanting glow.

As dawn approaches, shadows fade,
The silver coat in twilight laid.
Yet in the heart, the night remains,
A cherished song, a soft refrain.

## Dreamscapes in Frost

In twilight dreams where shadows play,
Frosted whispers guide the way.
The world asleep in icy grace,
Captured in a starlit space.

Crisp winds carry tales anew,
Of snowy lands and skies of blue.
Each flake a story, soft and light,
Weaving through the silent night.

Moonlit paths of shimmering white,
Call to wanderers of the night.
With every step, the magic flows,
In frosted realms, the spirit grows.

Beneath the hush of winter's breath,
Life dances lightly, defying death.
In frosty landscapes, dreams reside,
Where peace and wonder now abide.

Awake from dreams, the morning chimes,
But in the heart, the frost still shines.
A memory of night's embrace,
In dreamscapes lost, a timeless place.

# Beneath the Winter Moon

Beneath the moon's enchanting glow,
Whispers of winter softly flow.
The world adorned in white and grey,
As shadows dance, and night holds sway.

Frozen rivers whisper tales,
Of gentle winds and frosty trails.
Footprints mark the snowy ground,
In peaceful quiet, bliss is found.

Stars like lanterns twinkle high,
Guiding dreams as they drift by.
The frost-kissed air, a soothing balm,
Wrapped in the night, a perfect calm.

Trees stand tall in tranquil grace,
Guardians of this sacred space.
A hush falls over nature deep,
In winter's arms, all secrets keep.

As dawn approaches, shadows blend,
This magic night must soon descend.
Yet in each heart, the moonlight stays,
A whispered song of winter's days.

# A Serenade of Cold

In the chill of night, the echoes call,
A serenade of cold enthralls.
With every note, the frost takes flight,
In harmony with stars so bright.

Wind winds through the trees so tall,
A haunting tune, a whispered thrall.
Each breath a melody clear and pure,
Filling the soul, a spirit lure.

Snowflakes swirl like dancers fair,
Creating art in icy air.
With every step, a sound unfolds,
In winter's grasp, a tale retold.

Underneath the silver moon,
The serenade sings a gentle tune.
All nature breathes in tender sighs,
As cold embraces, softly lies.

As dawn's first light begins to break,
The world awakens, hearts now wake.
Yet in the stillness, we recall,
The serenade that shrouded all.

# A Tapestry of Winter's Embrace

Winds whisper through the trees,
A blanket white lays still,
Footprints fade in the soft snow,
Time pauses, moments spill.

Frosted breaths, a crystal song,
Nature's hush, a sacred rite,
Under stars, we weave our dreams,
Wrapped in winter's gentle light.

Icicles hang like silver threads,
Adorning branches, pure and bright,
The world transformed, a canvas fair,
In the arms of silent night.

Cups of cocoa, fireside glow,
Laughter dances in the air,
As shadows play on frosty walls,
Together, we banish despair.

Embrace the chill, let spirits soar,
For every breath brings life anew,
In this winter's tapestry,
Love blooms beneath skies so blue.

## Gleaming Crystals on Silent Paths

Beneath the moon, the world aglow,
Each step a crunch, a whispered sigh,
Crystals gleam on trails of white,
A frosty breath as time slips by.

Shadows dance on a frozen lake,
Stars twinkle in velvet dark,
Nature's jewels, a silent gift,
Walking paths where dreams can spark.

The air, a kiss of icy thrill,
Every exhale a fleeting jewel,
A secret whispered through the trees,
In winter's realm, we feel the cool.

Branches bow with a crystal crown,
Holding memories in icy grasp,
A silent promise in the night,
To cherish dreams we dare to clasp.

With every step, the heart will sing,
To chase the glimmer in the dark,
A world of wonder, vast and wide,
On silent paths, a fleeting spark.

## Nightfall in the Frozen Garden

In twilight's grip, the garden sleeps,
Crystals frosted on every leaf,
Whispers of night, a gentle breeze,
Wrapped in beauty, soft, and brief.

Moonlight drapes the world in silver,
A tranquil scene, so calm and clear,
Each flower bows, a frozen bloom,
Capturing dreams, holding them near.

The air has tales of yesteryear,
Traces of laughter, echoes bold,
As night enfolds the weary day,
In this embrace, we find our gold.

Stars above twinkle like gems,
A chorus of silence, sweet and bright,
In the garden's frozen heart,
We gather warmth amidst the night.

Though winter chills our wandering souls,
In the stillness, we feel alive,
A frozen garden, everlasting,
Where hopes and dreams forever thrive.

# The Quiet Symphony of Frozen Branches

Underneath the canopy of frost,
Branches sway in silent tune,
A symphony of winter's charm,
Beneath the soft embrace of moon.

Each flake that falls, a note so pure,
Dancing through the chilled night air,
Whispers of nature, soft and light,
In frozen beauty, we find care.

The world listens, as shadows play,
Time freezes in the stillness here,
Where echoes breathe a frosty hymn,
And every sigh is crystal clear.

Lullabies of winter's breath,
A melody we hold so dear,
In the quiet, we find our peace,
As nature sings, we draw it near.

The branches bow, a graceful dance,
In harmony with chilling breeze,
With every note, our hearts entwined,
In winter's symphony, we seize.

# Frost-Kissed Serenity

Morning light, soft and pale,
A world dressed in frosty veil.
Trees stand silent, cloaked in white,
Nature's beauty, pure and bright.

Gentle breath of winter's breeze,
Whispers through the swaying trees.
Stillness spreads, a tranquil sea,
In this moment, I am free.

Footprints crunch on icy ground,
In the silence, peace is found.
Each step forward, heart entwined,
With the stillness of my mind.

Frozen lake, a mirror clear,
Reflects the sky, so vast, so near.
In this haven, time stands still,
Every breath, a calming thrill.

As the sun dips low and red,
Painting skies where clouds once tread.
Frost-kissed dreams, softly sway,
In this serene, wintry play.

## Veiled in Winter's Whispers

Snowflakes fall like whispered dreams,
Each a tale, or so it seems.
Silent nights, where shadows wane,
Winter's song, both sweet and plain.

Barren branches, etched in frost,
Time slows down, too precious to cost.
Moonbeams dance on fields so wide,
A soft embrace that cannot hide.

Softly glowing, twilight glows,
Underneath the ice, life flows.
Each heartbeat within the cold,
A story waiting to be told.

Whispers carry through the night,
Crystallized in silver light.
Wrapped in warmth of winter's grace,
Frozen moments time can't erase.

In the hush of snowy streets,
Every echo gently greets.
Veiled in magic, pure delight,
Winter's heart, a precious sight.

## Moonlit Frost

Beneath the moon's soft, silver glow,
Frosty fields begin to show.
Nature whispers in the night,
With each flake, a twinkling light.

Stars adorn the endless sky,
As I walk, my thoughts can fly.
Echoes of the night surround,
In this stillness, peace is found.

Crystals glisten on the trees,
Dancing gently in the breeze.
Each breath taken, crisp and bright,
Wrapped in warmth, kissed by light.

Through the shadows, softly glide,
In this world, I take my stride.
Heartbeats match the moon's soft glow,
In frost's embrace, time moves slow.

As night deepens, dreams arise,
Underneath those starry skies.
Moonlit frost, a tranquil balm,
In this moment, everything's calm.

# Heartfelt Tranquility

In the stillness, I find peace,
As the winter's chill won't cease.
Breath like smoke in frosty air,
Heartfelt thoughts, my soul laid bare.

Gentle whispers of the night,
Guide me to that inner light.
Every corner of this place,
Wraps me in its soft embrace.

Twinkling stars, a distant song,
In this trance, I feel I belong.
Night unfolds, a sacred space,
Restful, calm, a sweet embrace.

Dreams like snowflakes softly fall,
Each one unique, they softly call.
Wrapped in warmth, I close my eyes,
Heartfelt dreams beneath the skies.

Breath of winter, pure and deep,
In this moment, I will keep.
Heartfelt tranquility shines bright,
Guiding me through the quiet night.

## Flickering Shadows Above a Frozen Canvas

On a canvas of pure white,
Shadows dance in muted light.
Every flicker tells a tale,
Of winter's chill and icy trail.

Crimson hues in fading sun,
Mark the day when warmth is done.
Night falls fast, the stars awaken,
In the frost, my heart unshaken.

Mysteries in shadows play,
Painting dreams that softly sway.
With each flicker, visions glide,
Through the night, my hopes reside.

Frozen breath on winter's air,
Brings a sense of deep despair.
Yet in silence, sparks ignite,
Flickering shadows, purest light.

Over fields of glistening snow,
Where the evening's whispers flow.
Every moment, a fleeting chance,
A frozen world, lost in dance.

# Silver Feathers from the Celestial Sky

Silvery whispers float down,
From stars in the vast unknown.
They dance on the breeze so light,
Kissing the earth goodnight.

Moonlit rays gently play,
Guiding dreams on their way.
Each feather tells a tale,
Of journeys that never fail.

Night blooms with soft delight,
Crafting shadows in the night.
Hope's glimmer shines so bright,
In the sky's eternal flight.

Floating softly through the air,
Finding hearts that truly care.
Such magic in every hue,
Silver threads connecting you.

In the silence of the night,
Stars gather for a new sight.
With each breath, they bestow,
Silver feathers from the glow.

## Velvet Hues in a Hushed Landscape

Wrapped in shades of deep velvet,
Nature's canvas, softly met.
Hues of mauve and midnight blue,
Whispering secrets just for you.

Underneath the moonlight's gaze,
Fields of dreams softly blaze.
Each petal, a story spun,
In the stillness, all is done.

The trees stand tall, wise and old,
Guardians of tales yet untold.
In their shade, shadows creep,
As the world around falls asleep.

A river flows with gentle grace,
Mirroring the sky's embrace.
In this hush, serenity lingers,
Touched by the night's soft fingers.

Velvet hues wrap the land tight,
Cradling both shadow and light.
In the silence, hearts will roam,
Finding in stillness a home.

# A Glimpse of Twilight in a Frosted Realm

Twilight paints the world aglow,
In frosty colors, soft and slow.
A whisper of dusk in the air,
Hints of magic everywhere.

Icicles dangle like crystal dreams,
Reflecting the sun's fading beams.
Every breath forms a frosty lace,
In the stillness, time finds its pace.

Trees wear coats of sparkling white,
Embracing the cool, crisp night.
In the hush, the cosmos sighs,
Underneath the twilight skies.

Footprints pressed in shimmering frost,
Tales of journeys never lost.
In this realm, where dreams take flight,
A glimpse of wonder shines so bright.

As shadows deepen and blend,
Frosted whispers softly send.
In this twilight, hearts will soar,
Craving just a little more.

## The Enchantment of Winter's Breath

Winter's breath, a chilly spell,
Wrapped in warmth, we know it well.
Each flake falls like whispered cheer,
A gentle hush, a time for dear.

Beneath the snow, the earth rests still,
Dreaming softly, against its will.
Nature holds its breath with grace,
In this enchanted, frosted space.

Fires crackle, shadows dance,
Inviting all to take a chance.
With every warmth that we create,
We gather hope, we celebrate.

The air is filled with scents divine,
Of cinnamon and pine, entwined.
In every corner, love takes leap,
As winter sings its song so deep.

With open hearts, together we share,
Moments wrapped in frosty air.
In the enchantment of this breath,
We find the beauty found in depth.

# A Canvas of White Under Cosmic Watch

Beneath the stars, the world is bright,
A canvas of white in the still of night.
Soft whispers of snow kiss the ground,
While the moon's gentle glow wraps all around.

Trees stand tall, dressed in winter's lace,
Nature's beauty, a serene embrace.
Footprints tread lightly, a moment so rare,
In silence, the cosmos watches and cares.

Each flake a story, unique in its fall,
In a world of wonder, there's magic for all.
Boundless the sky, with dreams interlace,
Under cosmic watch, we find our place.

## The Tranquility of the Winter Night

In the quiet of night, the world feels still,
A blanket of snow, an icy chill.
Stars twinkle softly, like distant dreams,
While the moon glows quietly, wrapped in beams.

Silence whispers secrets, nature's soft song,
As time slows down, righting the wrong.
Chill air carries whispers of long-lost lore,
In the tranquility, our spirits soar.

Frosted rooftops gleam under the starlight,
Each heartbeat echoes through the calm night.
Wrapped in warmth, we find our delight,
In the stillness of winter, everything feels right.

## Secrets Hidden in the Frost's Embrace

A veil of frost lays delicate and thin,
Hiding secrets deep, where stories begin.
Nature's own whispers behind icy glass,
In the chill of the morn, old memories pass.

Patterns unfold in a crystalline dance,
Each frozen breath holds a fleeting chance.
To glimpse at the past in the dawn's soft glare,
As the world awakens from dreams in the air.

Hidden whispers in the cold misty breath,
Capture the moments, a life after death.
As nature awaits, clothed in her white lace,
In the frost's embrace, we find a new grace.

## Starlit Reflections on Frosted Dreams

In the quiet of night, reflections appear,
Frosted dreams glisten, so crystal clear.
Stars look down, like eyes full of light,
Guiding our hopes through the velvety night.

Each breath we take, a cloud in the glow,
A dance of the heavens, with secrets to show.
Frozen landscapes stretch far and wide,
In the beauty of stillness, we find our guide.

Whispers of starlight, a gentle embrace,
In the heart of winter, we find our space.
Lost in the moment, where dreams take flight,
In starlit reflections, everything feels right.

## Serene Shadows of the Arctic Sky

Beneath the endless Arctic light,
Whispers of shadows take their flight.
Glistening ice and crystal air,
Silence wraps the world in care.

The northern winds begin to play,
A gentle waltz at close of day.
Stars twinkle high, a frosty show,
Illuminating the soft, white snow.

Auroras dance in vibrant hues,
Painting skies with greens and blues.
In this calm, the heart beats slow,
As nature's beauty ebbs and flows.

Silent mountains stand so tall,
Guardians of this icy hall.
The moonlight spills on fields of dreams,
In quietude, the spirit gleams.

Here in shadows, peace unfolds,
A tapestry of stories told.
In the Arctic night, we find,
A sanctuary for the mind.

## Enchanted Stillness in the Frosty Glow

In twilight's grip, the world stands still,
Frosty whispers, a soft thrill.
The stars above begin to gleam,
As nature drifts into a dream.

Covered paths in silver dust,
Silent trees in beauty trust.
Moonlight dances on the snow,
Casting shadows, a gentle glow.

Breath hangs in the biting air,
Every heartbeat, a sacred prayer.
Wrapped in warmth, the heart beats slow,
In this stillness, time won't go.

The silence sings a soothing song,
In enchanted realms, we belong.
Every flake that falls to ground,
Carves a magic, profound and round.

Whispers of the winter night,
Hold us close in softest light.
In the frost, our spirits play,
In enchanted stillness, we shall stay.

## A Winter's Heart Beneath the Stars

In the hush of a snow-cloaked night,
The universe shines, oh so bright.
A winter's heart begins to stir,
As cold winds through the pines confer.

Stars above, a shining thrill,
Nestled in the valley's chill.
Each twinkle holds a secret dream,
Reflecting on the icy stream.

The world beneath the skies so wide,
Finds solace in the winter's guide.
As snowflakes kiss the frozen earth,
Whispers of magic, a rebirth.

Beneath the frost, love takes its flight,
In the embrace of the starry night.
Hearts aglow with warmth and light,
A winter's charm, pure and bright.

Every breath, a cloud unfurls,
A dance of wonder that twirls and swirls.
In this realm where dreams ignite,
A winter's heart, a pure delight.

## The Magical Chill of a Still Evening

As twilight settles, the air grows cold,
Stories of winter gently unfold.
In the stillness, the world holds its breath,
A magical chill, a dance with death.

The stars awaken, one by one,
Glinting softly, like dreams begun.
Moonbeams spill on the sleeping ground,
In this peace, true magic is found.

Each breath creates a misty tale,
Wrapped in beauty, we shall not fail.
The chill of night, a sweet embrace,
In still evenings, we find our place.

Nature speaks in whispers low,
While shadows play and breezes blow.
Under the vast, enchanted sky,
Hearts are light, and spirits fly.

With every heartbeat, time slows down,
An evening's magic turns us around.
In a world at peace, we drift and sway,
Lost in the chill at the close of day.

# A Chill in the Air

The morning breathes a frosty sigh,
Whispers trace the winter sky.
Trees don cloaks of silver white,
As hearts seek warmth in quiet night.

Footsteps crackle on the ground,
Each echoing with a gentle sound.
Breath becomes small clouds of mist,
In this cold, the world is kissed.

Fires crackle, spirits high,
Gather close, let laughter fly.
The chill pulls tighter, bonds will form,
In the heart, we fight the storm.

Moonlight dances on the snow,
Guiding dreams, soft and slow.
Wrapped in layers, soft and dear,
We find comfort, ever near.

Night descends, a peaceful shroud,
Under stars, we feel so proud.
A chill lingers, yet we stay,
Together warming winter's play.

# Midnight Flurries

At midnight's gate, the flurries fall,
Whispering secrets, a siren's call.
Dancing softly on each street,
In this hush, the world feels sweet.

Stars peek through a cloudy veil,
As snowy shivers weave a tale.
Each flake unique, a fleeting grace,
In the dark, we find our place.

Crunching footsteps, laughter rings,
Under moonlight, the joy it brings.
Snowball fights and playful chase,
In cold's arms, we find our space.

The night wraps us in frosty light,
Breath escapes, a misty flight.
With every flurry falling down,
We wear warmth like a golden crown.

As dawn approaches, soft and bright,
The world transforms, pure delight.
With memories of each soft flurry,
We hold the night in gentle hurry.

## Celestial Cold Embrace

Underneath a starry dome,
The night unfolds, far from home.
A celestial cold embrace,
Whispers of a time and space.

Snowflakes twirl like dreams of old,
Each one glimmers, a tale retold.
In the stillness, hearts ignite,
Seeking warmth in the frosty night.

Galaxies in the distance shine,
Echoes of a cosmic line.
Underneath the icy glow,
We dance in rhythms soft and slow.

The universe sings in silence pure,
In winter's hold, we find a cure.
Wrapped in wonders, souls collide,
A fragile warmth we cannot hide.

With every breath, the cold invades,
Yet in this frame, the magic pervades.
In starlit nights, we learn to dream,
In celestial tides, love will beam.

## Echoes in the Frost

Among the trees where silence grows,
We walk where only nature knows.
Footsteps whispered in the frost,
In chilled air, warmth is not lost.

Echoes of laughter, memories shared,
In winter's grasp, love is declared.
Glimmers in the frost like stars,
In the stillness, we mend our scars.

Every flake a story spun,
To light our hearts, though day is done.
In this cold, our spirits blend,
In the frost, we find our friends.

The world can freeze in time and space,
Yet every heartbeat finds its place.
In echoes soft and shadows cast,
We're tied together, unsurpassed.

As the night deepens, we ignite,
With hopes and dreams, we take flight.
In echoes of the frosty night,
Love's warm glow will always light.

# Midnight's Slumbering Grace

In quiet night, the stars align,
A whispered breath, a gentle sign.
The shadows dance, the world at rest,
In dreams we find our hidden quest.

Soft silken sheets, embrace the soul,
While time stands still, it takes its toll.
Each heartbeat echoes, soft and slow,
In midnight's arms, we ebb and flow.

A lullaby sung by the moon's light,
Guiding us softly through the night.
In twilight's glow, we drift and sway,
As midnight cradles dreams away.

The breath of night, a sacred space,
We find our peace in slumber's grace.
Where burdens fade and silence reigns,
A world of dreams, where hope remains.

In ethereal skies, our spirits soar,
At dawn's first light, we long for more.
Midnight's slumbering grace, we keep,
Within our hearts, a promise steep.

# Trails of Moonlit Crystal

Winding paths, where shadows glint,
Beneath the trees, the stars imprint.
Across the fields, the whispers roam,
In moonlit glow, we find our home.

A silver sheen on every leaf,
The night unfolds, so calm, so brief.
Gentle breezes play a tune,
Melodies soft as the waning moon.

Footprints in frost, a fleeting trace,
Each step we take, a tender grace.
With every turn, the night reveals,
A hidden truth, our spirit heals.

The crystal gleams in mystic air,
A web of light, beyond compare.
In twilight's arms, we pause and see,
The trails of moonlit memories.

Boundless dreams beneath the sky,
In nature's arms, our worries die.
With every glance, the night invites,
A dance of shadows, soft moonlight.

## Silent Whispers in Frosted Air

In frosted air, the silence speaks,
With gentle sighs, the moonlight leaks.
A blanket white on earth's soft skin,
Where time stands still, and hope begins.

The world transformed, a crystal dream,
Where every shadow holds a gleam.
A hush envelops, crisp and clear,
As whispers float, we pause to hear.

Snowflakes dance on winter's breath,
Carving paths that lead to rest.
With every flake, a story spun,
In silent grace, two hearts are one.

Frozen landscapes, peace profound,
In stillness, love can often be found.
Together here, we hold the night,
In frosted whispers, pure delight.

Beneath the stars, we find our way,
In winter's grasp, forever stay.
Where silence reigns, our souls entwine,
In frosted dreams, your heart is mine.

# Moonlit Dreams on Winter's Chill

In winter's grasp, the moonlight glows,
A gentle touch on chilled repose.
With every breath, the night transforms,
As dreams take flight in velvet storms.

Crystalline paths beneath our feet,
In stillness, hearts begin to beat.
A silver sweep across the night,
Where whispers linger, soft and light.

The stars are veiled in hush of snow,
As moonlit dreams begin to flow.
With cozy warmth, we find our way,
In winter's chill, our hearts will stay.

Beneath the sky, the world so bright,
In frozen moments, love takes flight.
A tapestry of dreams we weave,
As we embrace what we believe.

In tranquil hours, our wishes soar,
On winter's breath, we ask for more.
With every glance, our souls will fill,
In moonlit dreams on winter's chill.

# Tread Softly on the Winter's Blanket

Gentle whispers in the snow,
Footprints linger, faint and slow.
Nature sleeps, a silent hymn,
Embrace the peace, let worries dim.

Branches bare, a crystal charm,
Each flake falls with a quiet calm.
Underneath the twilight's glow,
Heartbeats echo, soft and low.

Breath is visible, a fleeting sigh,
Winter's breath beneath the sky.
Stars above in silent pools,
Guiding night, where silence rules.

The world dressed in white, pure and bright,
Delicate dreams in the soft twilight.
Nature sings a lullaby sweet,
Tread softly on this winter's sheet.

With each step, a story unfolds,
In the frozen grasp, warmth beholds.
Remember well this tranquil time,
For winter's peace is pure and sublime.

## The Serene Glow of an Icy Night

In stillness wrapped, the night descends,
The icy glow, where magic blends.
Stars dance bright in a velvet sea,
Whispers carried on the breeze, so free.

Silhouettes of trees stand proud and tall,
Casting shadows on the snow's soft shawl.
Moonbeams glisten on the frozen ground,
A symphony of silence all around.

The breath of night, a chilly sigh,
Welcomes dreams as thoughts drift by.
Glistening frost on every edge,
Nature's art, a quiet pledge.

Each crystal holds a world inside,
Mirrors of wonder where secrets bide.
In the charm of an icy breath,
Life feels paused, as if in death.

The heart beats slow, a tender song,
In this moment, we all belong.
Underneath the winter's glow,
Feel the peace in the midnight snow.

## Frosted Illusions in the Moonlight

Silver shadows cast their spell,
In moonlit dreams, where secrets dwell.
Frosted whispers, soft and light,
Glimmering under the cloak of night.

Nature's canvas, crisp and bright,
Painted softly with pale moonlight.
Illusions dance on icy streams,
Breaking the silence with haunting dreams.

Beneath the stars, a world serene,
Every breath a fleeting scene.
Crystalline echoes fill the air,
Intricate patterns, a beauty rare.

Touch the frost with fingers cold,
Feel the magic, quiet and bold.
Moments captured in time's embrace,
In the stillness, find your place.

As dawn approaches, dreams will fade,
But memories linger, softly laid.
In the heart of night, reflect and feel,
Frosted wonders, forever real.

## Chilling Echoes in a Starlit Forest

Beneath the boughs, silence reigns,
Chilling echoes dance through the lanes.
A starlit path, both dark and bright,
Guides the wanderer through the night.

Whispers travel through the trees,
Carried softly on the breeze.
Each step echoes, sharp and clear,
In this hour, the night draws near.

Moonlight bathes the earth in grace,
Crafting shadows, a hidden place.
Flickering lights, the ground aglow,
In forest depths, where secrets flow.

The chill wraps close, like a veil,
Each heartbeat syncs with the night's tale.
Dreams entwined with the winds that sigh,
In the quiet, we learn to fly.

As stars twinkle in their cosmic dance,
Every heartbeat holds a chance.
To find our way in the silent dark,
In chilling echoes, we leave our mark.

# The Poetry of Icicles and Moonlight

Icicles hang like crystal strings,
Reflecting soft moon's glow,
Whispers of winter, they softly sing,
In shadows where chill winds blow.

Each drop that hangs, a story told,
Of frosty nights and glistening days,
A tapestry spun with threads so cold,
In nature's delicate, fleeting ways.

Moonlight kisses the frozen stream,
Where silence dances, softly bright,
A world draped in a silver dream,
Awakens softly under starlit night.

Every flake that falls from skies,
Is poetry shaped by craft and art,
Creating beauty that never dies,
Entrancing the soul, touching the heart.

Beneath this spell of icy grace,
The world holds its breath in delight,
In harmony, we lose our place,
As icicles shimmer in pale moonlight.

# Underneath the Shimmering Veil of Winter

Underneath the shimmering veil,
Winter whispers secrets low,
A blanket of white where dreams set sail,
In frosted fields, a world aglow.

Branches wear their coats of frost,
As night embraces day's retreat,
In nature's arms, nothing is lost,
Each echo of silence, bittersweet.

The stars peer down from heaven's dome,
While shadows weave through snowflakes bright,
In this stillness, we find a home,
Where hearts glow like embers, warm and light.

A tapestry spun with winter's breath,
Each moment held, both pure and rare,
In frozen realms, we dance with death,
Yet life remains, always aware.

Hushed horizons where dreams might rise,
Adorned with crystals that softly cling,
Beneath the blanket of silver skies,
Winter dances, a celestial king.

## A Ballet of Frost and Dreams

In the quiet of a winter's night,
Frosty figures twirl and glide,
Nature's ballet, pure delight,
Dreams entwined in snowflakes' ride.

Each breath of wind, a fleeting sigh,
While stars peek down with twinkling eyes,
A chorus of whispers in the sky,
And magic lives in soft goodbyes.

Moonlit shadows stretch and sway,
Painting stories on icy ground,
In this frosty ballet, we play,
In every twirl, our hearts are found.

The night is rich with wonder's grace,
As dreams take flight in silver light,
In nature's arms, we find our place,
Where dreams and frost meet in the night.

With every step, a tale unfolds,
Of whispered winds and gentle gleams,
In the chill, a warmth it holds,
A ballet of frost and vibrant dreams.

## Distant Echoes in a Frozen Silence

In the depth of a frozen night,
Echoes linger, soft and clear,
Whispers carried in the light,
Of memories that draw us near.

Silence reigns like a velvet cloak,
Wrapped around the sleeping earth,
Each footfall stirs not a stroke,
Of breezy tales or moments' worth.

Stars flicker like distant fires,
In the vast expanse, we feel the pull,
Of dreams woven with unseen wires,
In the tranquil void, ever full.

Frozen lakes hold secrets deep,
Reflecting shadows of the past,
In this stillness, spirits seep,
And in our hearts, their presence lasts.

Echoes fade into the mist,
Yet linger softly in the air,
In winter's grasp, we still persist,
Finding solace, finding care.

## The Calm Before the Frosted Dawn

A hush blankets the sleeping ground,
Whispers of dreams in shadows found.
The chill of night holds breath in pause,
Awaiting the light for nature's cause.

Stars twinkle softly, a celestial guide,
As winter's grip begins to slide.
A symphony of silence then unfolds,
Tales of beauty and warmth retold.

Frosted trees wear crystal crowns,
Each branch adorned in icy gowns.
The world holds its wisdom, calm and deep,
In the quiet moments before we leap.

A gentle glow begins to spread,
Kissing the earth, waking the dead.
The horizon blushes with a tender hue,
As daylight edges in, bold and new.

In that calm, we find our peace,
Nature's pulse, a sweet release.
Breathe in the stillness, embrace the dawn,
The frost will melt, but hope lives on.

## Midnight Murmurs in a White World

The midnight hour whispers low,
In a white world, where shadows glow.
Soft murmurs dance on the winter air,
Caressing hearts without a care.

Blankets of snow, so gently laid,
Carpets to soft freedom, unafraid.
Footsteps echo, a rhythmic beat,
Secrets shared where silence meets.

Moonlight spills on frosted streams,
A silver sheen that softly gleams.
Nature holds its breath tonight,
Wrapped in a cloak of purest white.

Crystalline branches, twinkling bright,
Cradle the dreams of soft twilight.
The whispers stir, both near and far,
Silent stories beneath the stars.

In this world, where time stands still,
Joy and tranquility softly fill.
Midnight murmurs wrap us tight,
In a white world bathed in starlit light.

## Frozen Petals in the Starlight

Petals drift in a quiet grace,
Frozen whispers of nature's embrace.
Under stars, they softly lie,
Beneath the blanket of a velvet sky.

Cascading ice, a jeweled tear,
Frame the beauty that draws us near.
Each bloom trapped in winter's clutch,
A fragile touch that means so much.

The world is still, a timeless pause,
Caught in wonder over nature's laws.
Starlight weaves through the crystal air,
Dancing gently with love and care.

In frozen gardens, dreams awake,
Petals glisten, like stars on a lake.
With every glimmer, hope ignites,
In silent nights of breathtaking sights.

So linger here in starlit grace,
Embrace the beauty that time can't erase.
For every frozen petal we see,
Holds a story of what's yet to be.

# An Arctic Waltz as Night Falls

As night falls softly on the ice,
The world sways to a gentle vice.
An arctic waltz begins to play,
Where silence dances, bright and gray.

Snowflakes twirl in the chilly breeze,
Spinning dreams with effortless ease.
Moonlit shadows glide in time,
To the rhythm of nature's rhyme.

Glistening layers in a frosty embrace,
The earth adorned, a magical place.
Each flake a note, a whispered grace,
Painting the dark with soft lace.

In this realm, the stars conspire,
To light our hearts, setting them afire.
As the night unfolds, we find our song,
A melody of peace where we belong.

So sway with joy, embrace the chill,
Let the arctic waltz the silence fill.
In the stillness, feeling free,
This night awakens the music in me.

## Whispers of Warmth Amidst the Cold

In the hush of winter's breath,
A flicker of hope ignites.
Soft whispers reach the frost,
Embracing the quiet nights.

Gentle hearts in cozy nooks,
Gather close as embers glow.
The world outside can freeze and bite,
But here, warmth and love will flow.

Frosty branches bend and sway,
A tapestry of white and gray.
Yet in our hearts, a flame withstands,
A bond that winters cannot fray.

Through the darkness, shadows creep,
Yet together, we find our light.
Each laughter shared rings like a bell,
A promise that holds tight and bright.

So here we sit, in cheer and glee,
Against the chill, we stand so bold.
With every hug and whispered word,
Amidst the cold, our warmth unfolds.

## Celestial Glow in a Frozen Wonder

Stars adorn the velvet night,
Their glimmer dances on the snow.
Each crystal flake a whispered tale,
Of magic that the skies bestow.

Moonlight bathes the land in dreams,
Illuminating frozen streams.
The world is hushed beneath its glow,
In this wonder, hearts take wing.

Twinkling lights among the trees,
Nature's canvas, vast and clear.
A silent choir sings to the night,
As warmth and hope draw ever near.

With every sigh of frosty air,
The universe unfolds its charm.
In this frozen wonderland,
There lies a peace that keeps us warm.

So let us wander hand in hand,
Beneath this celestial embrace.
In the glow of stars so bright,
We find our solace, our safe space.

# Twilight's Caress on a Glacial Night

As twilight spills its muted hues,
The world turns soft and still.
A tranquil hush blankets the earth,
In winter's tender thrill.

Shadows stretch like whispered dreams,
Draping valleys, hills, and trees.
Eve's quiet breath brings calm and peace,
A moment's magic, pure as breeze.

The frozen lake reflects the sky,
Mirroring the calm so deep.
In this serene and glacial night,
Nature's secrets softly seep.

The stars awaken, one by one,
Their brilliance adds to evening's grace.
Each twinkle tells a story clear,
Of all the worlds in distant space.

We linger here in twilight's arms,
Wrapped tightly in the evening's plea.
Embraced by dusk and shimmering light,
Glacial, yet so warm and free.

## Luminescence in the Deep Winter

When winter blankets all in white,
The world seems wrapped in dreams.
Yet in the depths of frigid nights,
A hidden glow forever gleams.

Softly lighting up the dark,
A spark ignites the endless frost.
Whispers of warmth rise from the hearth,
In quiet moments, we are lost.

The branches glisten, twinkling bright,
Each crystal captures every glance.
In winter's heart, a life still thrives,
Inviting us all to join the dance.

Beneath the cold, a pulse beats strong,
Life's essence lingers in the air.
With every breath, we fill our souls,
Finding warmth through every care.

In this deep winter, we will shine,
After shadows, we will rise.
For luminescence knows no bounds,
It blooms where love and courage lies.

# Crystal Starlight

Beneath the night, the crystals glow,
Stars twinkle softly, a cosmic flow.
Whispers of dreams in the frosty air,
A celestial dance, a moment rare.

The world asleep in slumber deep,
Heartbeats echo, a lullaby's keep.
Each flicker tells of tales untold,
In crystal starlight, magic unfolds.

Frozen whispers curl on the breeze,
Nature's song through the shivering trees.
A canvas dark where the dreams ignite,
All lost in the wonder of crystal light.

Time gently pauses, a breath in space,
Under the stars, we find our place.
Together we wander, shadows entwined,
In a world enchanted, souls aligned.

So let us cherish this dazzling night,
Under the cover of shimmering light.
With every heartbeat, we feel the spark,
Guided by hope through the endless dark.

# When the World Turns White

The dawn arrives with a snowy mask,
Each flake a secret, a wondrous task.
Fields enveloped in purest white,
Immaculate beauty, a stunning sight.

Footsteps crunch on the frozen ground,
In silence deep, a magic found.
Trees stand tall, draped in their shroud,
Whispers carried by the wind, proud.

Children laugh, their joy expands,
Building snowmen with eager hands.
A world transformed into a dream,
When the sun fades, and stars gleam.

The moonlight dances on snowy hills,
Nature's stillness, a heart that thrills.
In every corner, wonders grow,
As twilight spreads its silver glow.

When morning comes, the white remains,
A gentle calm that softly reigns.
For in this world, we've come to know,
In winter's grip, our spirits flow.

# Shrouded in Luminescence


Glimmers of light in the evening haze,
Illuminate paths in a gentle daze.
Shrouded in mystery, the night unfolds,
Stories of old in the glow retold.

Fireflies dance, a flickering grace,
Guiding lost souls to a sacred place.
Each spark a promise, a wish set free,
In the hush of the night, we find the key.

Moonlit rivers weave silver thread,
Candles flicker, where shadows tread.
Breath of the night whispers in our ears,
Banishing doubts, soothing our fears.

Beneath the stars, we gather close,
Shrouded in luminescence, we toast.
To dreams unspoken, our hearts unite,
In the embrace of the starry night.

The dawn will break, yet for now we stay,
Captivated by night, we drift away.
Bound by the magic, forever we roam,
In luminescence, we feel at home.

# Fables of the Frozen Ground

Whispers of winter in tales profound,
Echo through valleys of frozen ground.
Legends carved in the ice and snow,
Fables of old where the wild winds blow.

Once there were giants who danced with glee,
Their laughter ringing from tree to tree.
But as seasons changed, they faded away,
Leaving behind just stories to stay.

Each flake that falls holds a voice from the past,
A memory wrapped in the chill so vast.
In silence we listen, the echoes resound,
These are the fables of frozen ground.

Dreamers and wanderers gather near,
Around the fire, they share and hear.
The warmth of the flame, the chill of the night,
In fables told, we find our light.

As dawn breaks slowly, the tales will wane,
But the spirit of winter, it will remain.
For in every heart, a story is bound,
In the fables we weave on this frozen ground.

## Silvery Footprints in Stillness

In the quiet night, shadows play,
Silvery footprints guide the way.
Whispers of secrets in the air,
Stillness wraps around with care.

Moonlight dances on the leaves,
Nature's magic gently weaves.
Every step a story told,
In the hush, our dreams unfold.

Stars above, a shimmering sea,
Cloaked in silence, wild and free.
Echoes of laughter trail behind,
In the stillness, peace we find.

Time stands still beneath the sky,
Footprints fade, yet spirits fly.
In this moment, hearts align,
Silvery footprints, yours and mine.

As dawn breaks with vibrant light,
Memories linger, bold and bright.
In the stillness, love remains,
Through silvery footprints, joy sustains.

# Winter's Veil of Dreams

Snowflakes fall like whispered dreams,
Shrouding earth in gentle beams.
Winter's breath, a soft embrace,
Blanketing the world in grace.

Trees stand tall in silver-white,
Taunting stars that pierce the night.
Crystal chandeliers adorn,
Every branch, a crown reborn.

The chill ignites a spark of cheer,
Fires crackle, hearts draw near.
In cozy nooks, stories flow,
Winter's magic starts to grow.

Echoes of laughter fill the air,
Children playing without care.
Sleds and snowmen, vibrant sights,
Winter's glow ignites our nights.

As seasons turn, and memories blend,
Winter's tales will never end.
Wrapped in warmth, our dreams take flight,
Together through the starry night.

# A Night Wrapped in Wonder

Underneath a velvet sky,
Stars awaken, shining high.
The moon wears a silver crown,
Casting dreams across the town.

Night owls call from ancient trees,
Whispers carried by a breeze.
Mysteries dance in shadows deep,
A night where wonders softly leap.

Glistening dew on blades of grass,
Magic moments come to pass.
Every heartbeat, every glance,
In the dark, we dare to dance.

Lanterns flicker, hearts ignited,
In this hour, souls delighted.
Hand in hand, we wander far,
Underneath the guiding star.

As dawn approaches, dreams take flight,
But memories linger, pure delight.
Forever wrapped in wonder's bliss,
A night we'll cherish, not to miss.

## The Frost's Gentle Kiss

Morning light on frosted panes,
Nature dons her crystal chains.
A gentle kiss, the earth awakes,
In shimmering hues, a beauty makes.

Grass adorned in glistening white,
Dancing softly in the light.
Every blade a prism bright,
Whispers of a winter's night.

Breath comes forth in clouds of air,
Frosty fingers linger there.
In this stillness, hearts connect,
Moments paused in warm respect.

The world transforms in icy grace,
Each step a dance, a soft embrace.
Nature's art, a fleeting muse,
The frost, a gift we gladly choose.

As day evolves and shadows play,
Each fleeting sparkle fades away.
Yet in our hearts, this warmth persists,
Forever held, the frost's soft kiss.

## Secrets of a Frozen Horizon

Whispers ride the gentle breeze,
Underneath the frozen trees.
Secrets hide in snowflakes' fall,
Echoes dance, a silent call.

Moonlight glistens on the ice,
Casting dreams that feel so nice.
Footprints lost in wreaths of white,
Each step taken fades from sight.

Beneath the stars, a world anew,
Frozen whispers tell of truths.
Nature weaves its mystic lore,
In quietude, we seek for more.

Each glance towards that distant glow,
Holds the warmth of tales we know.
In the night, soft shadows play,
Painting thoughts that drift away.

Secrets rustle in the air,
In the cold, they whisper fair.
Journey on, where dreams take flight,
In the hush of winter's night.

## Luminary Nights

Stars awaken in velvet skies,
Shimmering like ancient eyes.
Moonlight dances, soft and bright,
Guiding hearts through the night.

Each flicker, a story told,
Of dreams and wishes, brave and bold.
In the stillness, we find peace,
As luminary lights increase.

Whispers linger on the air,
Magic woven everywhere.
Starlit paths lead us afar,
To discover who we are.

Night unfolds with gentle grace,
Stars illuminate every place.
Each heartbeat resonates within,
A cosmic dance, where souls begin.

Underneath the vast expanse,
We lose ourselves in starlit trance.
With every glance toward the sky,
We chase the dreams that never die.

## Thoughts Adrift on Winter Winds

Cold winds sweep across the plain,
Carrying whispers of the rain.
Thoughts adrift on frosty air,
Floating softly, free from care.

Branches sway, a gentle sway,
Nature's song in pure ballet.
Clouds drift slowly, gray and white,
Painting shadows in the light.

Each gust holds a fleeting thought,
Memories of battles fought.
In the silence, wisdom grows,
Caught in winter's tender throes.

Like leaves swirling through the trees,
Our wishes float upon the breeze.
Letting go of what we hold,
In the chill, we feel so bold.

Winter winds, so wild and free,
Guide our hearts, let us see.
Thoughts eternal, drifting on,
In the dusk, we find the dawn.

# The Quietude of Crystalline Dreams

In the hush of winter's grace,
Crystalline dreams find their place.
Gentle snowflakes tumble down,
Covering the world in gown.

Silence reigns, a soft embrace,
Time suspends in this still space.
Luminescent, stars align,
Reflecting thoughts, pure and divine.

Each moment whispers secrets deep,
In the quiet, promises keep.
Frozen echoes, bring to light,
The calm that dwells in starry night.

Dreams awaken, slowly rise,
Painting visions in the skies.
Life unfolds with every breath,
In serene whispers, dance with death.

Crystalline visions flow like streams,
In the silence, we find dreams.
Wrapped in warmth, we gently sway,
In the quietude, we find our way.

# Winter's Starry Inkwell

In the deep of night it glows,
A canvas vast, where starlight flows.
Each twinkle writes a tale anew,
Of whispered dreams in frosty blue.

The moon dips low, a silver pen,
It sketches softly as winter's den.
With every breath, the world complies,
In the stillness, magic lies.

A flurry dances on frozen sheets,
The stars above, they hum and greet.
Each glimmer sparkles, a fleeting sigh,
In winter's arms, where wishes fly.

The silence wraps each fallen snow,
In winter's chill, we come to know.
A longing heart, a quiet thrill,
In the ink of night, it's quiet still.

As dawn awakens, the colors blend,
In the starry inkwell, dreams ascend.
With every hue, the day will start,
Together spun, we share a heart.

# Hushed Footsteps on White

Softly creeping through the night,
Hushed footsteps whisper, pure and light.
Each step a secret, gently told,
In snow's embrace, the world is cold.

Blankets white on every street,
A muffled world beneath my feet.
Each print a story, each path a line,
In winter's realm, we intertwine.

Trees stand naked, arms held high,
Kissing clouds and dreams that fly.
Beneath the moon, shadows blend,
Where silence dwells and time can mend.

Breath in tendrils, warm and white,
Painting pictures in the night.
The stars above, a watchful eye,
On the hushed whispers as they sigh.

Every corner, a tale unfolds,
In the snow, a history holds.
As dawn will break and colors clash,
In winter's light, the moment's flash.

## The Stillness of Icebound Air


In the quiet of the frozen morn,
A breath held tight, like dreams reborn.
The world around, so crystal clear,
In icebound air, you feel it near.

Every sigh is a soft refrain,
Echoing within the gentle strain.
Nature pauses to catch its breath,
In the stillness, life feels the depth.

Frosted whispers on the trees,
Dancing lightly in the breeze.
The sky wears gray, its cloak so grand,
In icy silence, we take a stand.

Footprints trace where we have been,
Stories scattered, thin as skin.
The chill embraces, a soothing grip,
In winter's hush, we dream and sip.

Time feels slow; it gently bends,
In moments shared, the heart transcends.
Beneath the ice, a spark ignites,
In stillness, find the warm delights.

## Shadows Dance in the Snow

Underneath the midnight glow,
Shadows gather, twirl, and flow.
In the soft embrace of starlit night,
They waltz with secrets, hidden from sight.

Footprints trace the lines of grace,
Shapes that flicker, a soft embrace.
In moonlit gleam, they sway and spin,
Where whispered tales of winter begin.

As flakes descend, they swirl and play,
The quiet stars will guide their way.
Each movement whispers a silent call,
In winter's hush, they captivate all.

A tapestry spun of shadow and snow,
Dancing softly, come and go.
In the cold air, they gently weave,
A story told, for hearts that believe.

When dawn arrives with colors bright,
Shadows fade, but hold the night.
Yet in the heart, they'll dance again,
In winter's embrace, where dreams remain.

# Frosted Pathways

Step softly on the frozen ground,
Where whispers of winter can be found.
Each breath a cloud, each step a grace,
Nature's stillness, a quiet embrace.

Trees wear coats of glistening white,
Their branches bow, a splendid sight.
Footprints trace stories old and new,
In this sparkling realm, adorned in dew.

Moonlight dances on the icy stream,
Inviting hearts to pause and dream.
The world, a canvas, pure and bright,
Awakens wonder in the night.

Echoes of laughter, children play,
In frosty fields where spirits sway.
With every twirl, joy fills the air,
A tapestry woven with love and care.

So tread the pathways, soft and slow,
Embrace the chill, let your heart grow.
In winter's arms, we find delight,
A journey cherished, a pure respite.

## Stars Sparkling on White

Snowflakes fall in gentle descent,
Blanketing earth with a pure intent.
A shimmering coat, so fresh, so bright,
Stars sparkling softly in the night.

Every glimmer tells a tale,
Of frosty winds in a moonlit gale.
The world transformed, in silence bound,
Magic lingers, all around.

Crisp air bites, but we wear smiles,
As winter's charm spreads across miles.
With every step on this glistening floor,
Hearts grow warm with love's encore.

In this wonderland, spirits are free,
Dancing beneath the grand old tree.
Each branch a stage for moonlight's play,
As time drifts softly, then slips away.

So let us gather, hand in hand,
In this frosted, enchanted land.
Stars above in the velvet night,
Remind us all, of pure delight.

# Encased in Silence

A world encased in stillness sleeps,
Under a blanket that softly weeps.
Snow falls gently, embracing all,
As nature whispers, heeding the call.

Frost creeps slowly on window panes,
Painting memories, and quiet gains.
The air hangs thick with dreams unsaid,
In frozen moments, hopes are bred.

Footsteps echo in the misty dawn,
Through meadows white, where dreams are drawn.
Each breath a story, each pause a song,
In winter's hold, where hearts belong.

Silhouettes linger, shadows play,
In this hushed land, still night meets day.
The stars twinkle like distant sighs,
Guardians of wishes, in quiet skies.

So nestle close, seek warmth and light,
In this serene, silver-clad night.
For in stillness, beauty takes flight,
And dreams unfurl in the soft moonlight.

# A Tapestry of Frosted Light

Weaving threads of silver and white,
A tapestry born of the cold, crisp night.
Nature's brush strokes, soft yet bold,
Crafting wonders for hearts to behold.

Each flake a marvel, unique in form,
Dancing gracefully, weathering the storm.
Under the glow of a distant star,
The earth transforms, both near and far.

Trees stand guard, in their frosted attire,
Sheltering secrets of winter's choir.
Branches entwined, a delicate lace,
Holding the warmth of a tender embrace.

Children create, laughter abounds,
Building dreams on the snowy grounds.
Snowmen rise, with coal for their eyes,
Shimmering smiles under vast, open skies.

So let every heart, in this moment, unite,
In a dance of joy, a symphony bright.
For in this tapestry of frost and light,
We find our hopes, taking flight.